The

PAUL JOHNSON

A Phoenix Paperback

First published in Great Britain in 1987 by Weidenfeld & Nicolson
A Division of Orion Books Ltd
Orion House, 5 Upper St Martin's Lane, London WC2H 9EA

This abridged edition, published in 1996 by Phoenix, contains pages 482
to 517 of *A History of the Jews*.

ISBN 1 85799 525 2

Typeset by Deltatype Ltd, Ellesmere Port, Cheshire
Printed in Great Britain by Clays Ltd, St Ives plc

There was nothing inevitable about the capture of power in Germany by an anti-Semitic regime. But once Hitler had consolidated his personal and party dictatorship, which took a mere eight weeks in February--March 1933, a systematic attack on the Jews was certain. In particular, Jewish writers, artists and intellectuals knew he would go for them, and most of them left the country quickly. As a result Hitler actually killed fewer Jewish members of the intelligentsia than Stalin did in Russia. Strictly speaking, however, the Nazi policy for the Jews went no further than a reversion to conventional state anti-Semitism. The 1920 party policy provided for Jews to be stripped of German citizenship, including the right to hold office and vote; Jews would become 'guests', and those who had entered since 1914 would be expelled; there was also a vague threat to expropriate Jewish property. But in many of his speeches, as well as in *Mein Kampf*, Hitler had threatened and promised violence against Jews. In a private talk with Major Josef Hell in 1922 he went further. If he won power, he said, 'The annihilation of the Jews will be my first and foremost task. . . . Once the hatred and the battle against the Jews are really stirred up, their resistance will inevitably break down in short order. They cannot protect themselves and no one will stand forth as their defenders.' He explained to Major Hell his belief that all revolutions, like his, needed a focus of hostility, to express

1

'the feelings of hatred of the broad masses'. He had chosen the Jew not merely out of personal conviction but also out of rational political calculation: 'the battle against the Jews will be as popular as it will be successful'. The conversation with Hell is particularly illuminating because it illustrates the dualism of Hitler's anti-Semitic drive, its mixture of emotional loathing and cool reasoning. He treated Hell not only to his rationale but also to his fury:

I shall have gallows erected, in Munich for example in the Marienplatz, as many as traffic permits. Then the Jews will be hanged, one after another, and they will stay hanging until they stink. . . . As soon as one is untied, the next will take his place, and that will go on until the last Jew in Munich is obliterated. Exactly the same thing will happen in the other cities until Germany is cleansed of its last Jew.

Hitler's dualism expressed itself in two forms of violence to be used against the Jew: the spontaneous, highly emotional, uncontrolled violence of the pogrom, and the cool, systematic, legal and regulated violence of the state, expressed through law and police power. As Hitler moved closer to office, and became more adept at the tactics needed to secure it, he pushed the emotional element into the background, and stressed the legal. One of the chief complaints against Weimar was the political lawlessness on the streets. One of Hitler's chief attractions, to many Germans, was his promise to end it. But Hitler, long before he came to power, had mobilized instruments to express both aspects of his anti-Semitic personality. On the one hand there were the party street-bullies, and in particular the Brownshirts (SA), over 500,000 strong by the end of 1932, who habitually beat up Jews in the streets and even murdered them from time to time. On the other hand there was the elite ss, to run the police power and the camps, to administer the elaborate apparatus of state violence against the Jews.

During Hitler's twelve years in power, the dualism remained throughout. Right to the end, Jews were the victims both of sudden, individual acts of thoughtless violence, and of systematic state cruelty on a mass-industrial basis. During the first six years, in peacetime, there was a regular oscillation between the two. Once war imposed its own darkness and silence, the second gradually became predominant, on an enormous scale. It is true that Hitler was an improviser, a tactician of genius, who often reacted to events. True, also, that the scope of his persecution became so wide and varied as to develop a momentum of its own. Nevertheless, there was always a decisive degree of overall strategy and control, which came from no other mind but his, and expressed his anti-Semitic nature. The Holocaust was planned; and Hitler planned it. That is the only conclusion which makes sense of the whole horrifying process.

When Hitler first took power, his anti-Jewish policy was constrained by two factors. He needed to rebuild the German economy quickly. That meant avoiding the disruption inherent in the immediate dispossession and expulsion of the wealthy Jewish community. He wished to rearm as fast as possible. That meant reassuring international opinion by avoiding scenes of mass cruelty. Hence Hitler adopted the methods used against the Jews in fourteenth- and fifteen-century Spain. Individual acts of violence were promoted and encouraged, then used as pretexts to introduce formal, legal measures against the Jews. Hitler had agents for his dual purpose. Josef Goebbels, his propaganda chief, was his rabble-rousing Vicente Ferrer. Heinrich Himmler, head of the ss, was his cool, implacable Torquemada. Under the impulse of Goebbels' oratory and media, attacks on Jews by Brownshirts and party members, boycotts and terrorizing of Jewish businesses, began soon after Hitler took power. Hitler let it be known that he disapproved of these 'individual actions', as they were termed. But he left them unpunished, and he allowed them to build up into a climax in the summer of 1935. Then, in a major speech, he used them to justify the introduction of the Nuremberg Decrees on 15 September. These effectively carried out the original 1920 Nazi programme by stripping the Jews of their basic rights and beginning the process of separating them from the rest of the population. It was a reversion to the medieval system at its worst. But because it was a return to the odious but familiar past, it deceived most Jews (and the rest of the world) into believing that the Nuremberg system would give the Jews some kind of legal and permanent, albeit lowly, status in Nazi Germany. What they overlooked was the accompanying warning by Hitler, in the same speech, that if these arrangements for a 'separate, secular solution' broke down, then it might

4

become necessary to pass a law 'handing over the problem to the National Socialist Party for final solution'. In fact the instrument for this alternative was already being assembled. Himmler had opened his first concentration camp, at Dachau, only seven weeks after Hitler took over and he had since collected into his hands control over a repressive police apparatus which had no parallel outside Stalin's Russia.

On the plinth of the Nuremberg laws, an ever-growing superstructure of regulations restricting Jewish activity was progressively erected. By the autumn of 1938 the economic power of the Jews had been destroyed. The German economy was again strong. Germany was now rearmed. Over 200,000 Jews had fled from Germany. But the Anschluss with Austria had added as many Austrian Jews to the total. So the 'Jewish problem' remained unresolved, and Hitler was ready to move on to the next stage: its internationalization. If Jewish power in Germany had been destroyed, the power of the Jews abroad, and especially their power to make war upon him, became a growing theme of his speeches. The new dimension was dramatically personalized on 9 November 1938 when a Jew, Herschel Grynszpan, murdered a Nazi diplomat in Paris. This gave Hitler the pretext to move on to the next stage, using his dualist technique and both his agents. The same evening Goebbels told a meeting of Nazi leaders in Munich that anti-Jewish revenge riots had already started. On his suggestion, Hitler had decided that, if the riots spread, they were not to be discouraged. This was taken to mean that the party was to organize them. There followed the Kristall-nacht. Party members smashed and looted Jewish shops. The SA sent out teams to burn down all synagogues. The SS got the news at 11.05 p.m. Himmler minuted: 'The order was given by the propaganda directorate, and I suspect that Goebbels in his craving for power, which I noticed long ago, and also in his empty-headedness, started this action just at a time when the foreign political situation is very grave. . . . When I asked the Führer about it, I had the impression that he did not know anything about these events.' Within two hours he had ordered out all his police and SS forces to prevent large-scale looting and to take 20,000 Jews into the concentration camps.

There is little doubt that Hitler, whose orders on important matters were always oral, gave contradictory ones to Goebbels and Himmler. That was very characteristic. But there was an element of confusion as well as planning in this episode. It was used, as Hitler intended, to take further measures against Jews. They were held responsible for the riot, and fined a billion marks (about $400 million). But most of the cost of the damage had to be borne by insurance companies. There were a great many legal consequences. Jewish claims for damages in the courts had to be quashed by a special Justice Ministry decree. Cases against twenty-six party members accused of mur-dering Jews had to be quashed too. Four others who had raped Jewish women had to be expelled, and a distinction made between 'idealistic' and 'selfish' offences. Most disturbing of all, from Hitler's point of view, was that the pogrom was unpopular, not merely abroad but above all in Germany.

Hence he changed his tactics. Goebbels continued his anti-Semitic propaganda, but henceforth he was denied an executive role in anti-Jewish violence. That was now entrusted to Himmler almost entirely. As before, the 'outrage' was used as the pretext for a fresh campaign of legal measures against Jews. But this time the process was made highly bureaucratic. Every move was carefully thought out beforehand by experienced officials, not party theorists, and was made legal and systematic. As Raul Hilberg, the leading historian of the Holocaust, shows, it was this very bureaucratization of the policy which made possible its colossal scale and transformed a pogrom into genocide.

It also ensured that, at one time or another, almost every department of the German government, and large numbers of civilians, were involved in anti-Jewish activities. Hitler's war against the Jews became a national effort. To carry through the policy, the Jews had first to be identified, then dispossessed, then concentrated. Identification involved both the medical profession and the churches. The Nazis found that in practice it was too difficult to define a Jew by race. They had to fall back on religious criteria. Their basic decree of 11 April 1933, needed to throw Jews out of the civil service, defined a 'person of non-Aryan descent' as someone with a parent or grandparent of the Jewish religion. But this led to disagreements. In 1935, a medical conference between Dr Wagner, Chief Medical Officer of the party, Dr Blome, Secretary of the German Medical Association, and Dr Gross, head of the Race Political Office, decided that quarter-Jews were Germans but half-Jews were Jews, since (said Blome) 'among half-Jews the Jewish genes are notoriously dominant'. But the civil service would not accept this definition. They defined Jews as religious half-Jews or those married to Jews. The civil servants got their way because they actually wrote the detailed legislation, including the Reich Citizenship Law of 14 November 1935. Some twenty-seven race-decrees were written at the Interior Ministry by a former customs official, Dr Bernhard Losener, used to making fine distinctions between dutiable goods. Those applying for a wide range of jobs had to produce positive proof of Aryan descent. An ss officer had to produce proof of descent going back to 1750, but even a junior clerk in a government office needed seven authenticated documents. The churches, who had the only records of birth before 1875–6, were thus drawn in. A new profession of *Sippenforscher*, family researcher, was created. A third race of part-Jews, the *Mischling*, came into being, sub-divided into first and second degrees. Demands for reclassification, or 'liberation' as it was termed, multiplied, and as in Tsarist Russia the system led rapidly to every kind of nepotism and corruption. An official in Hitler's Chancellery, whom he liked but who was a second-degree *Mischling*, received a 'liberation' from the Führer, as a personal Christmas present, while he and his family were sitting round the tree on Christmas Eve 1938.

8

Again, dispossession of Jews, or Aryanization as it was called, brought a large section of the business community into the system. From August 1935, a Boycott Committee, which included Himmler and Streicher, and had all the resources of the state behind it, brought pressure to bear on Jews to sell out and to reduce the sale-price so that Germans could be induced to buy quickly. The banks played a prominent part in this, making a profit at every stage and often ending up with the business themselves. This was part of the process whereby German business was corrupted into taking part in the Final Solution. It was not just a question of benefiting from evil laws. Hitler's dualistic approach was used at every stage. Jews were stripped of their property by thuggery as well as law. IG Farben and the Deutscher Bank swallowed up the Österreichische Kreditanstalt and its industrial subsidiaries, after one of its top men was taken for a ride by the SA and thrown from a moving car, and another kicked to death by the SA during a search of his house. Baron Louis Rothschild was arrested by the police and held as a hostage until the family agreed to be dispossessed of their property at a knock-down price. Afterwards the Dresdner Bank wrote to Himmler's chief of staff thanking the police for help in bringing down the price.

The process of concentrating the Jews, cutting them off from the rest of the population and subjecting them to a completely different regime, also involved the nation as a whole. It was a very complicated and difficult process and demanded a degree of cold-blooded cruelty on the part of scores of thousands of bureaucrats which was almost as

9

pitiless as the eventual killing process itself. Moreover, all Germans were aware of it. Some anti-Jewish regulations were not published in the press. But everyone could see that Jews got different and inferior treatment in every aspect of life. After the Kristallnacht the sex and marriage laws became increasingly severe and were savagely enforced. A Jew caught 'fraternizing' with an Aryan was automatically sent to a concentration camp. The Aryan might be sent there too, for three months' 're-education'. At the same time, November 1938, Jews were expelled from all schools, and trains, waiting-rooms and restaurants were segregated. The shifting of Jews into segregated housing-blocks also began. Some of these actions were in accordance with elaborate decrees. Others had no legal basis at all. From start to finish, Hitler's war against the Jews was a bewildering mixture of law and lawlessness, system and sheer violence. From December 1938, for instance, Himmler reduced Jewish mobility, to assist the concentration process, simply by revoking all Jewish driving licences on his own authority. As the Jews were stripped of their property, they flocked into the big cities. The Jewish relief agencies, similarly impoverished, could not cope. So, under a decree of March 1939, unemployed Jews were pushed into forced labour.

Hence, by the opening of the war in September 1939, many of the eventual horrors had already been foreshadowed, and the system to carry them out was already in embryonic existence. Nevertheless, the war made a difference in two essential ways. First, it changed the emphasis of the moral justification for persecuting Jews which Hitler produced. This moral reasoning, crude though it might be, was an important element in the Holocaust because it was used publicly by Goebbels to secure the acquiescence or indifference of the German people, and by Himmler to promote the enthusiasm of those who manned the repressive machine itself. Until the outbreak of war, the argument ran that, since the Jews had been engaged for generations in defrauding the German people, they had no moral right to their property, and the measures to strip them of it were merely an act of simple restitution, their wealth going back whence it came – to the Reich. With the war, a new argument was added. Hitler had always insisted that, if a war came, it would be the work of the Jews, acting on the international stage; and when it did come, he held the Jews responsible for all the deaths that ensued. The conclusion implicit in this argument was that the Jews had no moral right to their lives either. Indeed he said on a number of occasions that war would precipitate a 'final solution' of the 'Jewish problem'.

This brings us to the second consequence of war. The experience of government, 1933–9, had led Hitler to modify his views on the popularity of anti-Semitism. It was useful to focus hatred, in the abstract, but he had learned that open, widespread, physical violence against the Jews as a whole was not acceptable to the German people, at any rate in peacetime. War, however, brought its own exigencies, and it also drew a veil over many activities. It was the necessary context in which genocide could be committed.   11

So far from the Jews creating the war, then, it was rather Hitler who willed the war in order to destroy the Jews. Not just German Jews either, but all European Jews, thus providing an international and final solution to what he had always claimed was an international problem. Not only was war necessary, to provide the pretext and concealment the act required; it had to include war against Poland and Russia, to give Hitler access to the principal source of European Jewry.

Hence with the opening of the first phase of the war, pressure on the Jews was rapidly increased. From September 1939 they had to be off the streets by 8 p.m. Then their movements were restricted in all areas at certain times, and in some areas at all times. They were banned from many forms of public transport except at certain inconvenient hours, or at any time. They were deprived of telephones, then forbidden to use them: phone booths were marked 'Use by Jews Forbidden'. Special Jewish identity papers went back to August 1938 and with the coming of war were made the basis for new systems of deprivation. Ration cards were stamped 'J' for deprivation-use in all kinds of ways. From December 1939 Jewish rations were cut, and at the same time Jews were restricted to certain shopping hours. One of Hitler's obsessions was that the First World War had been lost on the Home Front by food shortages often caused by Jewish rackets. He was determined that, this time, no Jew should eat a mouthful of food more than was necessary, and the Ministry of Food played a major part in his anti-Jewish policy. Indeed the bureaucrats there took progressively more severe measures designed, in effect, to starve the Jews to death.

At the same time Jews were being worked to death. They were excluded from the protective provisions of German labour laws. German employers took advantage of this, abolishing holiday pay for Jews. In early 1940 all allowances for Jews were abolished by law. On October 1941 a separate labour code for Jews allowed employers, for instance, to work fourteen-year-old Jewish boys for unlimited hours. Jews were deprived of protective clothing, welders of goggles and gloves. From September 1941 all Jews aged six or over had to wear a Star of David, black with a yellow background, as large as the palm of the hand, with the word *Jude* in the middle. This was an identification system which made it much easier to detect Jews breaking the countless regulations, turned the entire German nation into a police force and participants in the persecution, and demoralized the Jews themselves.

The opening of the war also brought Hitler half Poland and over two million Polish Jews. Moreover, Poland was an occupied country and he could do more or less what he liked there. Again, Hitlerian dualism was applied. First there were 'spontaneous' individual attacks, though on a much larger and more brutal scale than in Germany. Thus over fifty Jews were shot to death in a Polish synagogue. The SS held whipping orgies: at Nasielsky, early in 1940, 1,600 Jews were flogged throughout the night. The German army, which disliked the SS, kept records of these incidents, and some have survived. These violent incidents led to demands for 'orderly' solutions, and these in turn to systematic persecution.

Hence on 19 September 1939, Hitler decided to incorporate much of Poland in Germany proper, move 600,000 Jews from there into a Polish rump called the 'General Government', and ghetto all Jews within it at convenient points along the railways. For good measure he gave orders to shift all Germany's Jews there too. This brought into play the German railway system, the Reichsbahn, with its 500,000 clerical and 900,000 manual workers. Without the railways, the Holocaust would not have been possible. With their deportation trains called Sonderzüge, and their special staff, the Sonderzuggruppe, which co-ordinated the deportation schedules with the rest of the war timetables, the railways made prodigious efforts to get the Jews exactly where the ss wanted them. These trains carrying Jews were given priority over everything else. When a ban on all other uses of railways was imposed in July 1942, during the 266-division offensive in Russia, the ss still ran a daily train carrying 5,000 Jews to Treblinka and a twice-weekly one of 5,000 to Belzec. Even at the height of the Stalingrad panic, Himmler wrote to the Transport Minister: 'If I am to wind up things quickly, I must have more trains for transport. . . . Help me get more trains!' The minister obliged him. Study of the train factor indicates, perhaps better than anything else, the importance of his Jewish policy in Hitler's overall scheme, and the extent to which ordinary Germans helped him to push it to its conclusion.

14   Once Jews were separated, mobilized and concentrated

in the General Government, what Hitler called (2 October 1940) *ein grosses polnisches Arbeitslager*, 'a huge Polish labour-camp', the forced-labour programme could begin in earnest. This was the first part of the Final Solution, of the Holocaust itself, because working to death was the basis on which the system operated. Fritz Saukel, the head of the Allocation of Labour Office, ordered that Jews were to be exploited 'to the highest possible extent at the lowest conceivable degree of expenditure'. The labourers were worked from dawn till dusk seven days a week, dressed in rags and fed on bread, watery soup, potatoes and sometimes meat scraps. The first major slave-labour operation was in February 1940, the construction of a vast anti-tank ditch along the new eastern frontier. Thereafter the system spread to every area of industry. Workers could be 'ordered' by phone and shipped by freight-car just like raw materials. Thus IG Farben got 250 Dutch women Jews freighted from Ravensbrück to Dachau, the same freight-cars taking back 200 Polish women to Dachau. Slave workers were usually forced to move at the double, the 'Auschwitz Trot', even when carrying, for example, bags of concrete weighing 100 lb. At Mauthausen, near Hitler's home town of Linz, where Himmler built a work-camp near the municipal quarry, labourers had only picks and axes, and they had to carry heavy chunks of granite up 186 steep and narrow steps from the quarry to the camp. They had a life expectancy of between six weeks and three months, and this did not include death by accident, suicide or punishment.

There is no doubt at all that forced labour was a form of murder and regarded as such by the Nazi authorities. The words *Vernichtung durch Arbeit*, 'destruction through work', were used repeatedly in discussions which Dr Georg Thierack, the Minister of Justice, had with Goebbels and Himmler on 14 and 18 September 1942. Rudolf Höss, the commandant at Auschwitz May 1940–December 1943, and afterwards office chief at the Main Security Headquarters from which the entire anti-Jewish programme was directed, testified that by the end of 1944 400,000 slaves were working in the German armaments industry. 'In enterprises with particularly severe working conditions', he said, 'every month one-fifth died or were, because of inability to work, sent back by the enterprises to the camps in order to be exterminated.' So German industry was a willing participant in this aspect of the Final Solution. The labourers had no names – just numbers, tattooed on their bodies. If one died, the factory manager did not have to state the cause of death: he merely asked for a replacement. Höss testified that the initiative in securing Jewish slave labour always came from the firm: 'The concentration camps have at no time offered labour to the industry. On the contrary, prisoners were sent to firms only after the firms had made a request for [such] prisoners.' All the companies concerned knew exactly what was happening. Nor was the knowledge confined to very senior managers and those involved in the actual slave-labour operations. There were innumerable visits to the camps. In a few cases written reactions have been preserved. Thus one IG Farben employee, visiting the Auschwitz slave-labour operation, 30 July 1942, wrote to a colleague in Frankfurt, using the tone of joking irony which many Germans adopted: 'That the Jewish race is playing a special part here you can well imagine. The diet and treatment of this sort of people is in accordance with our aim. Evidently an increase of weight is hardly ever recorded for them. That bullets start whizzing at the slightest attempt of a "change of air" is also certain, as well as the fact that many have already disappeared as a result of a "sunstroke".'

Yet starving and working the Jews to death was not quick enough for Hitler. He determined on mass killing too, in the spirit with which he had discussed it with Major Hell. Signed orders from Hitler of any kind are rare, and rarest of all are those dealing with the Jews. The longest letter Hitler ever wrote about Jewish policy goes back to spring 1933, in reply to a request from Hindenberg to exempt war veterans from anti-Jewish decrees. The absence of written orders led to the claim that the Final Solution was Himmler's work and that Hitler not only did not order it but did not even know it was happening. But this argument will not stand up. The administration of the Third Reich was often chaotic but its central principle was clear enough: all key decisions emanated from Hitler. This applied particularly to Jewish policy, which was the centre of his preoccupations and the dynamic of his entire career. He was by far the most obsessively and fundamentally anti-Semitic of all the Nazi leaders. Even Streicher, in his view, was taken in by the Jews: 'He *idealized* the Jew,' Hitler insisted in December

1941. 'The Jew is baser, fiercer, more diabolical than Streicher depicted him.' Hitler accepted anti-Semitic conspiracy theory in its most extreme form, believing that the Jew was wicked by nature, was indeed the very incarnation and symbol of evil. Throughout his career he saw the 'Jewish problem' in apocalyptic terms and the Holocaust was the logical outcome of his views. His orders to set it in motion were oral but were invariably invoked by Himmler and others as their compelling authority, according to regular formulae: 'the Führer's wish', 'the Führer's will', 'with the Führer's agreement', 'this is my order which is also the Führer's wish'.

The decisive date for the Final Solution was almost certainly 1 September 1939, when hostilities began. Hitler had stated plainly, on 30 January that year, what his reaction to war would be: 'if international-finance Jewry inside and outside Europe should succeed once more in plunging the nations into yet another world war, the consequences will not be the Bolshevization of the earth and thereby the victory of Jewry, but the annihilation [*Vernichtung*] of the Jewish race in Europe.' He regarded the war as his licence for genocide and he set the scientific process in motion the very day war broke out. The first programme, of experimental murder, was conceived in Hitler's Chancellery and the original order went out on Hitler's personal stationery on 1 September 1939: this authorized the murder of the incurably insane. The programme was code-named T-4 after the Chancellery address, Tiergartenstrasse 4, and from the start it had the characteristics of the genocide programme: ss involvement, euphemism, deception. It is significant that the first man appointed to head the euthanasia programme, ss Obergruppenführer Dr Leonard Contin, was sacked when he asked for written orders from Hitler. He was replaced by another ss doctor, Philip Boyhaler, who accepted oral orders.

The ss experimented with various gases, including carbon monoxide and the cyanide-based pesticide tradenamed Zyklon-B. The first gas chamber was set up at a killing centre in Brandenburg in late 1939, Hitler's doctor, Karl Brandt, witnessing a test killing of four insane men. He reported back to Hitler, who ordered only carbon monoxide to be used. Five other killing centres were then equipped. The gas chamber was called a 'shower-room' and the victims, taken in groups of twenty or thirty, were told they were to have a shower. They were sealed in, then the doctor on duty gassed them. This was the same basic procedure later used at the mass-extermination camps. The programme murdered 80,000–100,000 people, but was stopped in August 1941 following protests by the churches – the only occasion when they prevented Hitler from killing people. But by this time it was also being used to kill Jews from concentration camps who were too sick to work. So the euthanasia programme merged into the Final Solution, and there were continuities in methods, equipment and expert personnel.

It should be emphasized that the killing of large numbers of Jews continued in Poland throughout 1940 and the spring of 1941, but the mass-extermination phase did not really begin until Hitler's invasion of Russia, 22 June 1941. This was designed to destroy the centre of the Jewish–Bolshevik conspiracy and to give Hitler access to the five million Jews then under Soviet control. Killing was done by two methods: mobile killing units, and fixed centres or death camps. The mobile killing system dates back to 22 July 1940 when Hitler's idea of total war, involving mass extermination, was first presented to the army. Indeed, the army was heavily involved in the Final Solution since the SS killing units came under its command for tactical purposes. An entry on 3 March 1941 in General Jodl's War Diary records Hitler's decision that, in the coming Russian campaign, SS Police units would have to be brought right up to front-line army areas in order to 'eliminate' the 'Jewish–Bolshevik intelligentsia'.

This was the origin of the Einsatzgruppen, the mobile killing battalions. They were directed from the Reich Security Main Office (RHSA) under Reinhard Heydrich, the chain of command going Hitler–Himmler–Heydrich. There were four such battalions, A, B, C and D, each 500–900 strong, assigned to each of the four army groups invading Russia. They had a high proportion of high-ranking officers drawn from the SS, Gestapo and police, and included many intellectuals and lawyers. Otto Ohlendorf, who commanded D, had degrees from three universities and a doctorate in jurisprudence. Ernst Biberstein, one of the commanders in C, was a Protestant pastor, theologian and church official.

Of the Jews in Soviet territory, four million lived in areas overrun by the German army 1941–2. Of these two and a half million fled before the Germans arrived. The rest was 90 per cent concentrated in the cities, making it easier for the Einsatzgruppen to kill them. The murder battalions moved directly behind the army units, rounding up Jews before the city populations knew what was in store. In the initial killing sweep, the four groups reported at various dates between mid-October and early December 1941 that they had killed 125,000, 45,000, 75,000 and 55,000 respectively. But many Jews were left behind in the rear areas, so killing teams were sent to catch and murder them. The army co-operated in handing them over, salving its conscience by referring to Jews as 'partisans' or 'superfluous eaters'. Sometimes the army killed Jews themselves. Both they and the SS incited pogroms, to save themselves trouble. There was little resistance from the Jews. Russian civilians were co-operative, though there is one recorded act of a local mayor shot for trying 'to help the Jews'. Quite small groups of killers disposed of enormous numbers. In Riga, one officer and twenty-one men killed 10,600 Jews. In Kiev, two small detachments of C killed over 30,000. A second sweep began at the end of 1941 and lasted throughout 1942. This killed over 900,000. Most Jews were murdered by shooting, outside the towns, at ditches turned into graves. During the second sweep, mass graves were dug first. The killers shot the Jews in the back of the neck, the method used by the Soviet secret police, or by the 'sardine method'. Under this, the first layer stretched themselves at the bottom of the grave and were killed from above. The next layer lay down on top of the first bodies, heads facing the feet. There were five or six layers, then the grave was filled in.

Some Jews hid under floorboards and in cellars. They were blasted out with grenades or burned alive. Some Jewish girls offered themselves to stay alive; they were used during the night but killed all the same the next morning. Some Jews were only wounded and lived hours, even days. There were many sadistic acts. There was reluctance too, even among these picked killers, to slaughter so many people who put up no resistance – not a single member of any of the groups died during an actual killing operation. Himmler paid only one visit to see the work, witnessing 100 Jews shot in mid-August 1941. There is a record of it. Himmler found himself unable to look as each volley rang out. The commander reproached him: 'Reichsführer, those were only a hundred.' Himmler: 'What do you mean by that?' 'Look at the eyes of the men in this *Kommando*. How deeply shaken they are! These men are finished for the rest of their lives. What kind of followers are we training here? Either neurotics or savages.' Himmler then made a speech to the men, calling on them to obey 'the Highest Moral Law of the Party'.

To escape from the degree of personal contact between killers and killed involved in shooting, the groups tried other methods. The use of dynamite proved disastrous. Then they introduced mobile gas vans, and soon two were sent to each battalion. Meanwhile, these mobile killing operations were being supplemented by the use of fixed centres, the death camps. Six of these were built and equipped: at Chelmno and Auschwitz in the Polish territories incorporated in the Reich; and at Triblinka, Sobibor, Majdanek and Belzec in the Polish General Government. In a sense, the term 'death camp' as a special category is misleading. There were 1,634 concentration camps and their satellites and more than 900 labour camps. All were death camps, in that enormous numbers of Jews died there, by starvation and overwork, or by execution for trivial offences or often for no reason at all. But these six camps were deliberately planned or extended for mass slaughter on an industrial scale.

Hitler seems to have given the orders for mass extermination in fixed centres in June 1941, at the same time as the mobile killing units went into action. But as we have seen, large-scale killing by gas was already taking place; and in March 1941 Himmler had already instructed Höss, commandant at Auschwitz, to enlarge it for this purpose. It had been chosen, Himmler told him, because of its easy rail access and isolation from centres of population. Shortly afterwards, Himmler instructed Odilo Globocnik, ss-Police head in Lublin, to build Majdanek, and this official became head of a killing network which included two other death camps, Belzec and Sobibor. The chain of command was as follows. Hitler's orders went through Himmler, and from him to individual camp commanders. But Hermann Göring, as boss of the Four-Year Plan, was involved administratively in arranging the co-operation of various state bureaucracies. This is an important point, showing that, while the executive agent of the Holocaust was the SS, the crime as a whole was a national effort involving all the hierarchies of the German government, its armed forces, its industry and its party. As Hilberg put it, 'The co-operation of these hierarchies was so complete that we may truly speak of their fusion into a machinery of destruction.'

Göring delegated the co-ordinating role to Heydrich, who as head of the RSHA and Chief of Security Police was the junction of state and party, and sent him a written order, 31 July 1941:

As supplement to the task that was entrusted to you in the decree dated 24 January 1939, namely to solve the Jewish question by emigration and evacuation in the most favourable way possible, given present conditions, I herewith commission you to carry out all necessary preparations with regard to the organizational, substantive and financial viewpoints, for a total solution of the Jewish question in the German sphere of influence in Europe. In so far as the competences of other central organizations are hereby affected, these are to be involved.

Heydrich, in turn, gave orders to Adolf Eichmann, his RSHA official in charge of 'Jewish Affairs and Evacuation Affairs'. He had administrative responsibility for the Holocaust as a whole, though Himmler exercised operational responsibility through his camp commanders. It was Eichmann who actually drafted the 31 July 1941 order signed by Göring. But at the same time an additional oral order was given by

Hitler to Heydrich and transmitted to Eichmann: 'I have just come from the Reichsführer: the Führer has now ordered the physical annihilation of the Jews.'

Construction of the mass-killing machinery went on throughout the summer and autumn of 1941. Two civilians from Hamburg came to Auschwitz to teach the staff how to handle Zyklon-B, which was the preferred killing method there. In September, the first gassing was carried out, in Auschwitz Block 11, on 250 Jewish hospital patients and 600 Russian prisoners. Then work began on Birkenau, the main Auschwitz killing-centre. The first death camp to be completed was Chelmno, near Lodz, which started functioning on 8 December 1941, using exhaust gases from mobile vans. An RSHA conference on the killing had been planned for the next day, at a villa in the Berlin suburb of Wannsee. But it was postponed because of Pearl Harbor, and did not take place until 20 January 1942. By then there was a certain note of anxiety among the top Nazis. The survival of Russia, and the entrance of America into the war, must have convinced many of them that Germany was unlikely to win it. The conference was to reaffirm the object of the Final Solution and to co-ordinate means to carry it through. There was lunch, and while waiters handed round brandy, several present urged the need for speed. It was from this point on that the exigencies of the Holocaust were given priority even over the war effort itself, reflecting Hitler's resolve that, whatever the outcome of the war, the European Jews would not survive it.

Wannsee was followed by rapid action. Belzec became

operational the next month. The building of Sobibor began in March. At the same time Majdanek and Treblinka were transformed into death centres. Goebbels, after a briefing by Globocnik, in charge of the General Government camps, noted (27 March 1942): 'A judgment is being visited on the Jews [which is] barbaric. . . . The prophecy which the Führer made ˙about them for having brought on a new world war is beginning to come true in a most terrible manner.'

Goebbels, however, was confiding to his diary. In actual orders, even for a very limited circulation, the genocide was invariably described in euphemistic code. Even at the Wannsee conference, Heydrich used code. All Jews, he said, were to be 'evacuated to the East' and formed into labour columns. Most would 'fall away through natural decline' but the hard core, capable of rebuilding Jewry, could be 'treated accordingly'. This last phrase, meaning 'killed', was already familiar from Einsatzgruppen reports. There were many official euphemisms for murder, used by those within the operations and well understood by countless thousands outside them: Security Police measures, worked over in the Security Police manner, actions, special actions, special treatment, moved East, resettlement, appropriate treatment, cleansing, major cleansing actions, conveyed to special measures, elimination, solution, cleaning up, making free, finished, migration, wandering, wandered off, disappeared.

The euphemisms were considered necessary, even among the professional mass-killers, to minimize any brooding on the sheer enormity of what they were doing. There were about 8,861,800 Jews in the countries of Europe directly or indirectly under Nazi control. Of these it is calculated that the Nazis killed 5,933,900, or 67 per cent. In Poland, which had by far the largest number, 3,300,000, over 90 per cent, were killed. The same percentage was reached in the Baltic States, Germany and Austria, and over 70 per cent were killed in the Bohemian Protectorate, Slovakia, Greece and the Netherlands. More than 50 per cent of the Jews were killed in White Russia, the Ukraine, Belgium, Yugoslavia, Rumania and Norway. The six big death camps formed the main killing areas, murdering over two million at Auschwitz, 1,380,000 at Majdanek, 800,000 at Treblinka, 600,000 at Belzec, 340,000 at Chelmno and 250,000 at Sobibor. The speed with which their gas chambers worked was awesome. Treblinka had ten of them, each accommodating 200 people at a time. It was Höss's boast that at Auschwitz each of his gas chambers could take 2,000. Using Zyklon-B gas crystals, the five Auschwitz chambers could murder 60,000 men, women and children every twenty-four hours. Höss said that he murdered 400,000 Hungarian Jews alone (as well as other groups) during the summer of 1944, and that in total 'at least' 2,500,000 humans (Jews and non-Jews) were gassed and incinerated at Auschwitz, plus another half-million who died of starvation and disease. For many months in 1942, 1943, and 1944, the Nazis were each week killing in cold blood over 10,000 people, mainly Jews.

That atrocities on this scale could have been carried out

in civilized Europe, albeit in wartime and behind the protective screen of the German army, raises a number of questions about the behaviour of the German people, their allies, associates and conquests, about the British and Americans, and not least about the Jews themselves. Let us examine each in turn.

The German people knew about and acquiesced in the genocide. There were 900,000 of them in the SS alone, plus another 1,200,000 involved in the railways. The trains were one giveaway. Most Germans knew the significance of the huge, crowded trains rattling through the hours of darkness, as one recorded remark suggests: 'Those damned Jews, they won't even let one sleep at night!' The Germans were beneficiaries of murder. Scores of thousands of men's and women's watches, fountain-pens and propelling pencils, stolen from the victims, were distributed among the armed forces; in one six-week period alone, 222,269 sets of men's suits and underclothes, 192,652 sets of women's clothing, and 99,922 sets of children's clothes, collected from the gassed at Auschwitz, were distributed on Germany's Home Front. The recipients knew roughly where these came from. The Germans did very little to protest about what was being done to the Jews or to help Jews escape. But there were exceptions. In Berlin, at the very heart of Hitler's empire, several thousand of the city's 160,000 Jews managed to escape by going underground, becoming 'u-boats' as they were called: In each case it meant some connivance and assistance by non-Jewish Germans. One such was the scholar Hans Hirschel, who became a u-boat in February 1942. He moved into the flat of his mistress, the Countess Maria von Maltzan, sister-in-law of Field Marshal Walter von Reichenau, an ardent Nazi. She designed for him a box-like bed into which he could climb, with holes drilled for breathing. Each day she put in a fresh glass of water and a cough-suppressant. One day she came back to her flat and heard Hirschel and another U-boat, Willy Buschoff, singing at the top of their voices: 'Hear O Israel the Lord our God, the Lord is one'.

The Austrians were worse than the Germans. They played a role in the Holocaust out of all proportion to their numbers. Not only Hitler, but Eichmann and Ernst Kaltenbrunner, head of the Gestapo, were Austrian. In the Netherlands, two Austrians, Arthur Seyss-Inquart and Hanns Rauter, directed the killing of the Jews. In Yugoslavia, out of 5,090 war criminals, 2,499 were Austrian. Austrians were prominent in the mobile killing battalions. They provided one-third of the personnel of the SS extermination units. Austrians commanded four out of the six main death camps and killed almost half of the six million Jewish victims. The Austrians were much more passionately anti-Semitic than the Germans. Menashe Mautner, a disabled veteran of the First World War with a wooden leg, fell on the icy pavements of Vienna and lay there three hours vainly asking the passers-by for help. They saw his star and refused.

The Rumanians were no better than the Austrians; worse in some ways. There were 757,000 Jews in pre-war Rumania, among the worst treated in the world. The

Rumanian government followed Hitler step by step in his anti-Jewish policy, with far less efficiency but added venom. From August 1940, laws stripped Jews of their possessions and jobs and subjected them to unpaid forced labour. There were pogroms too – in January 1941 170 Jews were murdered in Bucharest. The Rumanians played a major part in the invasion of Russia which for them was also a war against the Jews. They killed 200,000 Jews in Bessarabia. Jews were packed into cattle-trucks without food or water and shunted around with no particular destination. Or they were stripped of their clothes and taken on forced marches, some actually naked, others dressed only in newspapers. The Rumanian troops working with Einsatzgruppe D in southern Russia outraged even the Germans by their cruelty and their failure to bury the corpses of those they murdered. On 23 October 1941 the Rumanians carried out a general massacre of Jews in Odessa, after a land-mine destroyed their army HQ. The next day they herded crowds of Jews into four large warehouses, doused them with petrol and set them alight: between 20,000 and 30,000 were thus burned to death. With German agreement, they carved out the province of Transnistria from the Ukraine, as their own contribution to the Final Solution. In this killing area, 217,757 Jews were put to death (an estimated 130,000 from Russia, 87,757 from Rumania), the Rumanians dispatching 138,957 themselves. After the Germans and Austrians, the Rumanians were the biggest killers of Jews. They were more inclined to inflict beating and torture, or to rape, the officers being worse than the men since they selected the prettiest Jewish girls for orgies. They were also more mercenary. After they shot Jews they sold the corpses to local peasants who stripped them of their clothes. They were willing to sell live Jews too if they could get enough cash for them. But from 1944 on their attitude became less bellicose as they realized the Allies would win.

In France too there was an important section of opinion willing to take an active part in Hitler's Final Solution. It had never forgiven the Dreyfusard victory in 1906 and its hatred of the Jews was reinforced by the Blum Popular Front government of 1936. As in Germany, the anti-Semites included a great many intellectuals, especially writers. They included a doctor, F. L. Destouches, who wrote under the pen-name Céline. His anti-Semitic diatribe, *Bagatelle pour un massacre* (1937), written under his real name, was highly influential just before and during the war, arguing that France was already a country occupied (and as a woman raped) by Jews, and that a Hitlerian invasion would be a liberation. This extraordinary book resurrected a deep-seated notion that the English were in unholy alliance with Jews to destroy France. During the Dreyfus case the phrase 'Oh Yes', pronounced in an exaggerated English accent, was an anti-Semitic war-cry, and in *Bagatelle* Céline lists the slogans of the Anglo-Jewish world conspiracy: 'Taratboum! Di! Yie! By gosh! Vive le Roi! Vivent les Lloyds! Vive Tahure! Vive la Cité! Vive Madame Simpson! Vive la Bible! Bordel de Dieu! Le monde est un lupanar juif!' There were no fewer than ten anti-Semitic political organizations in France, some of them funded by the Nazi government, calling for the destruction of the Jews. Mercifully they could not agree on a common policy. But their moment came when the Vichy government adopted an anti-Semtic policy. Darquier de Pellepoix, who had founded the Rassemblement Anti-Juif de France in 1938, became Vichy Commissaire-Général aux Questions Juifs in May 1942. Most of the French declined to collaborate with the Final Solution policy but those who did were more enthusiastic than the Germans. Thus Hitler contrived to kill 90,000 (26 per cent) of French Jews, and of the 75,000 deported from France, with the help of the French authorities, only 2,500 survived. There was a large element of personal hatred in French wartime anti-Semitism. In 1940, the Vichy and German authorities received between three and five million poison-pen letters denouncing particular individuals (not all of them Jews).

Hitler found his Italian ally much less co-operative. Since the end of the papal states, the Italian Jewish community had become one of the best-integrated in Europe. As King Victor Emmanuel III told Herzl (1904): 'Jews may occupy any position, and they do. . . . Jews for us are full-blown Italians.' It was also one of the oldest in the world. Benito Mussolini liked to joke that Jews 'supplied the clothes after the rape of the Sabine Women'. Jews had produced two Italian prime ministers and one war minister; they provided a disproportionately large number of university teachers, but also of generals and admirals. Mussolini himself oscillated all his life between philo-semitism and anti-Semitism. It was a group of Jews who helped to convert him to intervention in the First World War, the critical moment in his life when he broke with Marxist internationalism and became a national socialist. Five Jews were among the original founders of the *fasci di combattimento* in 1919 and Jews were active in every branch of the Fascist movement. The learned article on anti-Semitism in the *Fascist Encyclopaedia* was written by a Jewish scholar. Both Mussolini's biographer, Margharita Sarfatti, and his Minister of Finance, Guido Jung, were Jews. When Hitler came to power, Mussolini set himself up as the European protector of the Jew and was hailed by Stefan Zweig as '*wunderbar* Mussolini'.

Once the Duce fell under Hitler's spell his anti-Semitic side became uppermost but it had no deep emotional roots. There was a definite anti-Semitic fringe within the Fascist Party and government but it was much less powerful than in the Vichy regime and seems to have had no popular support at all. Italy, in response to German pressure, introduced race laws in 1938 and when war came some Jews were interned in camps. But it was not until the Italian surrender in 1943 delivered half of Italy into German military control that Himmler was able to draw it into the Final Solution. On 24 September he sent instructions to his ss boss in Rome, Herbert Kappler, that all Jews, irrespective of age or sex, were to be rounded up and sent to Germany. But the German ambassador in Rome, whose Italian mistress was hiding a family of Jews in her home with his approval, gave no help and the military commander, Field-Marshal Kesselring, said he needed the Jews to build fortifications. Kappler used his order to blackmail the Jewish community. There was a gruesome, medieval scene in the German embassy, where he saw its two leaders, Dante Almansi and Ugo Foa, and demanded 50 kilos of gold within thirty-six hours; otherwise 200 Jews would be murdered. The two men asked to be allowed to pay in lire but Kappler sneered: 'I can print as much of that as I want.' The gold was delivered to the Gestapo within four days. Pope Pius XII offered to provide as much as was needed but by this time enough had been collected, many non-Jews, especially parish priests, contributing. A more serious loss was the most valuable volumes of *Judaica* in the community library, which went to swell Alfred Rosenberg's private collection.

Himmler, who wanted live Jews to kill, not treasure, was furious with Kappler and sent his round-up expert, Theodor Dannecker, with a team of forty-four ss killers, to conduct a *Judenaktion*; he had carried out similar ones in Paris and Sofia. The German ambassador to the Holy See warned the Pope, who ordered the Rome clergy to open sanctuaries. The Vatican sheltered 477 Jews and a further 4,238 found refuge in convents and monasteries. The raid was a failure. Kappler reported: 'The anti-Semitic section of the people was nowhere to be seen during the action, only a great mass of people who in some cases tried to cut off the police from the Jews.' But it yielded 1,007 Jews, who were sent straight to Auschwitz and all but sixteen were murdered. There were raids in other Italian towns, also largely frustrated by the Italians. One notable survivor was

Bernard Berenson, the intensely bookish scion of a Lithuanian rabbinical family who, in a secular age, had become the world's leading authority on Italian Renaissance painting. He was tipped off in code by the local police. 'Dottore, the Germans want to come to your villa but we are not sure exactly where it is. Could you give us instructions for your visit tomorrow morning?' The Italians hid him for the rest of the German occupation.

In other European states, the ss got little or no help. But this did not necessarily mean failure in rounding up Jews. In occupied Greece, without any local help, they murdered all but 2,000 of the ancient 60,000-strong Salonika Jewry. In Belgium, despite local resistance, they killed 40,000 out of 65,000 Jews and almost wiped out the famous diamond-trading quarter of Antwerp. The ss effort in the Netherlands was particularly fierce and unremitting and, although the Dutch went so far as to hold a general strike to protect the Jews, the total loss was 105,000 out of 140,000. The Finns, Germany's ally, refused to yield up their 2,000 Jews. The Danes succeeded in ferrying almost their entire Jewish community of 5,000 into Sweden. On the other hand, the great Hungarian Jewry, the last to be sacrificed, lost heavily: 21,747 were murdered in Hungary, 596,260 were deported, of whom only 116,500 survived.

The mass murder of the Hungarians took place at a time when the Allies had complete air superiority and were advancing rapidly. It raised in acute, practical form the question: could the Allies have done anything effective to save European Jewry? The Russians were closest to the 35

Holocaust but never showed the slightest desire to help the Jews in any way. On the contrary: Raoul Wallenberg, the Swedish diplomat and humanitarian, who tried to save Jewish lives in Budapest, vanished when the Red Army arrived there, the Swedes being told: 'measures have been taken by the Soviet military authorities to protect Mr Raoul Wallenberg and his belongings'. He was never seen again.

The British and American governments were in theory sympathetic to the Jews but in practice were terrified that any aggressively pro-Jewish policy would provoke Hitler into a mass expulsion of Jews whom they would then be morally obliged to absorb. For the Nazis, emigration was always one element in the Final Solution, and although the balance of evidence seems to show that Hitler was determined to murder Jews rather than export them, he was quite capable of modifying his policy to embarrass the Allies if they gave him the opportunity. Goebbels wrote in his diary, 13 December 1942: 'I believe both the British and the Americans are happy that we are exterminating the Jewish riff-raff.' This was not true. But neither power was prepared to save Jewish lives by accepting large numbers of refugees. Of all the major European powers, Britain was the least anti-Semitic in the 1930s. Sir Oswald Mosley's Blackshirt movement, founded in 1932, was a failure, not least because it attacked Jews. The government feared, however, that widespread anti-Semitism would be the inevitable result of a mass immigration of Jews. Nor were they prepared to budge from the immigration restrictions laid down in the 1939 White Paper for Palestine. Winston

Churchill, always a Zionist, favoured a larger Jewish intake. But his Foreign Secretary, Anthony Eden, argued that to open up Palestine would alienate all Britain's Arab allies there and destroy her military position in the Middle East. When the New York Jewish leader Rabbi Stephen Wise asked him in Washington (27 March 1943) to support an Anglo-American plea to Germany to let the Jews leave occupied Europe, Eden told him the idea was 'fantastically impossible'. But he privately confessed: 'Hitler might well take us up on any such offer.' The Foreign Office were against taking Jews and resented even Jewish requests to this effect: 'A disproportionate amount of the time of this office', minuted one senior official, 'is wasted in dealing with these wailing Jews.'

The United States could certainly have accommodated large numbers of Jewish refugees. In fact during the war period only 21,000 were admitted, 10 per cent of the number allowed under the quota law. The reason for this was public hostility. All the patriotic groups, from the American Legion to the Veterans of Foreign Wars, called for a total ban on immigration. There was more anti-Semitism during the war than at any time in American history. The polls showed, 1938–45, that 35–40 per cent of the population would have backed anti-Jewish laws. In 1942, according to the polls, the Jews were seen as a bigger threat to America than any other group after Japanese and Germans. In 1942–4, for instance, every synagogue in New York's Washington Heights was desecrated. News of the extermination programme was available from May 1942, 37 when the Polish Jewish Labour Bund got verified reports to the two Jewish members of the Polish National Committee in London. This included descriptions of the gas vans at Chelmno and the figure of 700,000 Jews already murdered. The *Boston Globe* gave it the headline 'Mass Murders of Jews in Poland Pass 700,000 Mark' but buried the story on page 12. The *New York Times* called it 'probably the greatest mass slaughter in history' but gave it only two inches. In general the Holocaust news was under-reported and tended to get lost in the general wartime din of horror stories. But there was also great resistance in America to accepting the fact of the Holocaust, even when the US army broke into the camp areas. James Agee, writing in the *Nation*, refused to watch the atrocity films and denounced them as propaganda. The GIs were furious when people back home refused to believe what they had seen or even look at their photos.

A major obstacle to action was F. D. Roosevelt himself. He was both anti-Semitic, in a mild way, and ill informed. When the topic came up at the Casablanca Conference, he spoke of 'the understandable complaints which the Germans bore towards the Jews in Germany, namely that while they represented a small part of a population, over 50 per cent of the lawyers, doctors, schoolteachers, college professors in Germany were Jews' (the actual figures were 16.3, 10.9, 2.6 and 0.5 per cent). Roosevelt seems to have been guided purely by domestic political considerations. He had nearly 90 per cent of the Jewish vote anyway and felt no spur to act. Even after the full facts of systematic extermination became available, the President did nothing for fourteen months. A belated Anglo-American conference on the issue was held in Bermuda in April 1943, but Roosevelt took no interest in it, and it decided that nothing of consequence could be done. Indeed it specifically warned 'that no approach be made to Hitler for the release of potential refugees'. In the end, a War Refugee Board was created. It had little help from the government and 90 per cent of its funds came from Jewish sources. But it did contrive to save 200,000 Jews, plus 20,000 non-Jews.

The question of bombing the gas chambers was raised in the early summer of 1944, when the destruction of the Hungarian Jews got under way. Churchill in particular was horrified and keen to act. The killing, he minutes, 'is probably the greatest and most horrible crime ever committed in the whole history of the world'. He instructed Eden, 7 July 1944: 'Get anything out of the Air Force you can and invoke me if necessary.' An operation was feasible. An oil-refining complex 47 miles from Auschwitz was attacked no less than ten times between 7 July and 20 November 1944 (by which point the Holocaust was complete and Himmler ordered the death machinery to be destroyed). On 20 August 127 Flying Fortresses bombed the Auschwitz factory area less than five miles to the east of the gas chambers. Whether bombing would have saved Jewish lives cannot be proved. The ss were fanatically persistent in killing Jews, whatever the physical and military obstacles. It was certainly worth trying. But Churchill was its only real supporter in either government. Both the air forces hated military operations not directed to destroying enemy forces or war potential. The US War Department rejected the plan without even examining its feasibility.

Here we come to a harsh and important point. The refusal to divert forces for a special Jewish rescue operation was in accordance with general war policy. Both governments had decided, with the agreement of their respective Jewish communities, that the speedy and total defeat of Hitler was the best way to help the Jews. This was one reason why the vast and powerful US Jewish community gave little priority to the bombing issue. But once winning the war was accepted as the overriding objective, the Final Solution had to be seen in this perspective. And, for the Nazi war-effort, it was from first to last a self-inflicted wound. On the German side it was opposed by everyone, whether army or industrial chiefs, who took a rational view of the war. It occupied scores of thousands of military personnel. It often paralysed the railway system, even during critical battles. Most of all, it killed over three million productive workers. Many of these were highly skilled. Moreover, Jewish war-workers, knowing their likely fate, tried fanatically to make themselves indispensable to the war effort. There is a mass of evidence to show that all those Germans involved in production tried hard to keep their Jewish staff. To quote only one of many examples, the organizer of war factories in occupied Russia reported:

Almost insoluble was the problem of finding expert managers. Almost all former owners were Jews. All enterprises had been taken over by the Soviet state. The Bolshevik Commissars have disappeared. The Ukrainian trustee administrators [were] incompetent, unreliable and completely passive. . . . The real experts and real heads are Jews, mostly the former owners or engineers. . . . They try their utmost and extract the very last ounce of production, until now almost without pay, but naturally in the hope of becoming indispensable.

But of course all these Jews were killed. Hence the Holocaust was one of the factors which were losing Hitler the war. The British and American governments knew this. What they did not sufficiently appreciate was that the main military beneficiary of the Holocaust was the Red Army, and the ultimate political beneficiary would be the Soviet empire.

The Allied calculation might have been different if the Jews had produced a resistance movement. None emerged. There were many reasons for this. The Jews had been persecuted for a millennium and a half and had learned from long experience that resistance cost lives rather than saved them. Their history, their theology, their folklore, their social structure, even their vocabulary trained them to negotiate, to pay, to plead, to protest, not to fight. Then too, the Jewish communities, especially in eastern Europe, had been emasculated by many generations of mass migration. The most ambitious had gone to America. The most energetic, adventurous, above all the most militant, had gone to Palestine. This drain of the best and brightest had continued right up to the war and even during it. Jabotinsky had predicted the Holocaust. But the uniformed, trained, even armed Jewish groups in Poland were designed not to resist Hitler but to get Jews to Palestine. When war broke out, Menachem Begin, for instance, was escorting a group of 1,000 illegal emigrants across the Rumanian frontier on their way to the Middle East. So he got out too. That made sense. The fighting Jews wanted to make their stand in Erez Israel, where they had a chance, not in Europe, where it was hopeless.

The great mass of Jews who remained, overwhelmingly religious, were deceived and self-deceived. Their history told them that all persecutions, however cruel, came to an end; that all oppressors, however exigent, had demands that were ultimately limited and could be met. Their strategy was always geared to saving 'the remnant'. In 4,000 years the Jews had never faced, and had never imagined, an opponent who demanded not some, or most, of their property, but everything; not just a few lives, or even many, but all, down to the last infant. Who could conceive of such a monster? The Jews, unlike the Christians, did not believe the devil took human shape.

The Nazis, precisely to minimize the possibility of resistance, made pitiless use of Jewish sociology and psychology. In Germany they exploited the Jewish Gemeinde in each city, the Landesverbände in each region, and the Reichsvereinigung for the entire country, to get Jewish officials to do the preparatory work for the Final Solution themselves: to prepare nominal rolls, report deaths and births, transmit new regulations, set up special bank accounts open to the Gestapo, concentrate the Jews in particular housing blocks and prepare charts and maps for deportation. This was the model for the Jewish Councils in the occupied countries which unwittingly helped the Nazis push through the Final Solution. About 1,000 of these *Judenrate* were organized, involving 10,000 people. They were formed mainly out of the pre-war religious *kehillot* (congregational bodies). In the Soviet-occupied areas, all the bravest community leaders had already been shot before the Germans arrived. The Germans used the *Judenrate* to spot the actual or potential troublemakers and kill them instantly. Thus the Jewish leadership tended to be compliant, fearful and sycophantic. The Nazis used them first to despoil the Jews of all their valuables, then to organize bodies of Jews for forced labour and deportation to the killing centres. In return they were given privileges and power over their fellows.

The system was seen at its most odious and formidable in the biggest Polish ghettos, especially Lodz and Warsaw. The Lodz ghetto had 200,000 Jews crowded into it, with a living density of 5.8 a room. It was a killing centre in itself, 45,000 dying there of disease and starvation. The Warsaw ghetto had no less than 445,000 Jews, with a room-density of 7.2; there, 83,000 died of hunger and sickness in less than twenty months. Jews were concentrated in the ghettos, then funnelled out of them into the death trains. Internally, the ghettos were petty tyrannies, run by men like Chaim Mordechai Rumkowski, the strutting dictator of the Lodz ghetto, who even had his head printed on postage stamps. Their power was enforced by unarmed Jewish police (there were 2,000 in the Warsaw ghetto), supervised by Polish police, with the armed German Sip (security police) and the ss watching everyone. The ghettos were not wholly uncivilized. The Jewish social services worked to the best of their meagre resources. Secret *yeshivot* were organized. Warsaw, Lodz, Vilna and Kovno even had orchestras, though they were officially allowed to play only music by Jewish composers. There were clandestine newspapers printed and circulated. The Lodz ghetto, as befitted a medieval-type institution, had a chronicle. But there was never any doubt in the minds of the Germans about the function of the ghetto and its Jewish authorities. It was to make what contribution it could to the war effort (Lodz had 117 little war factories, Bialystok twenty) and then, when the deportation orders for the camps came, to ensure that the process was orderly.

To keep resistance to a minimum, the Germans lied at every stage of the process, and employed elaborate deceptions. They always insisted that deportations were to work-sites. They had postcards printed stamped Waldsee, which camp-inmates were made to send home, which read: 'I am well. I work and am in good health.' On the transit to Treblinka, they constructed a dummy station with a ticket office, hand-painted clock and a sign reading: 'In transit to Bialystok'. The death chambers, disguised as shower-rooms, had Red Cross markings on the doors. Sometimes the ss had all-inmate orchestras play music as the Jews were marshalled towards the 'shower-rooms'. The pretence was kept up until the end. A note found in the clothes of one victim reads: 'We arrived at the place after a long journey and at the front of the entrance is a sign "Bathhouse". Outside, people receive soap and a towel. Who knows what they will do with us?' At Belzec, 18 August 1942, an ss disinfectant expert, Kurt Gerstein, heard as ss officer chant, while naked men, women and children were pushed into the death chamber: 'Nothing is going to hurt you. Just breathe deep and it will strengthen your lungs. It is a way to prevent contagious diseases. It is a good disinfectant.'

The deception often worked because the Jews wanted to be deceived. They needed to have hope. The ss skilfully fed rumours into the ghettos that only a portion of Jews were required for deportation, and successfully sold the Jewish leadership the line that a maximum degree of co-operation produced the best chance of survival. The ghetto Jews were reluctant to believe in the existence of the extermination camps. When two young Jews escaped from Chelmno early in 1942 and described what they had seen there, it was argued that they had been unhinged by their experiences and their report was withheld from the underground press. Not until April, when reports from Belzec confirmed the Chelmno story, did the Warsaw Jews believe in the death machinery. In July the Warsaw ghetto boss, Adam Czerniakow, realizing he could not save even the children, took cyanide, leaving a note: 'I am powerless. My heart trembles in sorrow and compassion. I can no longer bear all this. My act will prove to everyone what is the right thing to do.' But even at this stage, many Jews clung to the hope that only some would die. Jacob Gens, the ghetto boss in Vilna, told a public meeting: 'When they ask me for a thousand Jews, I hand them over. For if we Jews do not give of our own, the Germans will come and take them by force. Then they will take not one thousand but many thousands. By handing over hundreds, I save a thousand. By handing over a thousand, I save ten thousand.'

Jewish religious training tended to encourage passivity. The hasidic Jews were the most ready to accept their fate as God's will. They quoted scripture. 'And thy life shall hang in doubt before thee; and thou shalt fear night and day, and shalt have no assurance of thy life.' They got into the death trains wrapped in their prayer-shawls, reciting the psalms. They believed in martyrdom for God's glory. If, by chance or God's mercy, they were spared, then it was a miracle. A whole collection of hasidic tales about the wondrous sparing of individual lives grew up during the Holocaust. One community leader noted: 'The truly pious have become even more pious, for they see God's hand in everything.' A member of the Jewish *Sonderskommando*, who cleared out the Auschwitz death chambers after a gassing, testified that he saw a group of pious Jews from Hungary and Poland, who had managed to get some brandy, dance and sing before entering the gas rooms, because they knew they were about to meet the Messiah. Other, more secular Jews also found joy and acceptance of God's will in the horror. The remarkable diaries which a Dutch-Jewish woman, Ettie Hillesum, kept in Auschwitz show that the tradition of Job lived on in the Holocaust: 'Sometimes when I stand in some corner of the camp, my feet planted on your earth, my eyes raised towards your heaven, tears run down my face, tears . . . of gratitude.'

As the ghettos were gradually emptied, some Jews did determine to fight, though political divisions delayed agreement on a plan. In Warsaw, under pretence of building air-raid shelters, the Jews constructed dug-outs connected to the sewer system. They were led by a twenty-four-year-old, Mordecai Anielewicz, who recruited 750 fighters and contrived to get possession of nine rifles, fifty-nine pistols and a few grenades. The Nazis decided to destroy the ghetto on 19 April 1943, using the Waffen-ss. By that time they were only 60,000 Jews left in it. In the desperate fighting that followed, mainly underground, they killed sixteen Germans and wounded eighty-five. Anielewicz was killed on 8 May, but the rest held out another eight days, by which time several thousand Jews were dead in the debris. Some European countries, with well-equipped armies, had not resisted the Nazis for so long.

There was even a revolt within Auschwitz itself on 7 October 1944. Jews working in a Krupp plant smuggled in explosives; they were turned into grenades and bombs by skilled Soviet POWs. The revolt itself was carried out by the Sonderkommando of Crematoria III and IV. They managed to blow up Crematorium III and kill three ss men. About 250 Jews were massacred by the guards, but twenty-seven escaped. Four Jewish girls who got the explosives in were tortured for weeks, but gave no information. Roza Robota, who died under torture, gave as her last message: 'Be strong and brave.' Two of them survived the torture to be hanged in front of all the women in Auschwitz, one of them with the cry 'Revenge!' as she died.

But as a rule there was no resistance at all, at any stage of the extermination process. The Germans always struck suddenly, with overwhelming force. The Jews were numb with terror and hopelessness. 'The ghetto was encircled by a large SS detachment,' wrote an eye-witness at Dubno (Ukraine),

and about three times as many Ukrainian militia. Then the electric arclights erected in and around the ghetto were switched on. . . . The people were driven out in such haste that small children in bed were left behind. In the street women cried out for their children and children for their parents. That did not prevent the SS from driving the people along the road at running pace, and hitting them until they reached the waiting freight-train. Car after car was filled, and the screaming of women and children, and the cracking of whips and rifle shots, resounded unceasingly.

Many Jews died on the trains, and when the survivors arrived they were hustled straight off to the death chambers. Kurt Gerstein watched, in the early morning, a trainload of 6,700 Jews arrive at Auschwitz in August 1942. There were 1,450 dead on arrival. He saw 200 Ukrainians, armed with leather whips, open up the freight-car doors, order out the living and beat them to the ground.
Loudspeakers screamed at them to strip naked. The hair

was brutally shorn from the heads of all females. Then the entire shipment, stark naked, were driven towards the gas chambers which they were told were 'disinfectant baths'. At no point did anyone have a chance to resist. The most they could do was to tear up the miserable crumpled dollars they had concealed on their persons, so that the Nazis would not have the use of them – their last and only gesture of protest.

No Jew was spared in Hitler's apocalypse. The Theresienstadt camp in Czechoslovakia, full of old people, was run to preserve the pretence that the Jews were merely being 'resettled'. To it were sent so-called privileged Jews, holders of the Iron Cross First Class or better, and 50-per-cent disabled war veterans. But of the 141,184 sent there, only 16,832 were alive when the camp fell to the Allies on 9 May 1945: more than 88,000, the old and the brave alike, had been gassed. No Jew was too old to be murdered. After the Anschluss, the friends of Freud, old and dying of cancer, had ransomed him from the Nazis and brought him to England. It did not occur to him, or to anyone, that his four elderly sisters, left behind in Vienna, were at risk. But they too were swept into the Nazi net: Adolfine, aged eight-one, was murdered in Theresienstadt, Pauline, eighty, and Marie, eighty-two, in Treblinka, Rose, eighty-four, in Auschwitz.

No Jew was too young to die. All women arriving at the death camps were shaved to the skin, the hair being packed up and sent to Germany. If a breast-fed baby was a nuisance during the shaving, a guard simply smashed its head against the wall. A witness at the Nuremberg trials testified: 'Only those who saw these things with their own eyes will believe with what delight the Germans performed these operations; how glad they were when they succeeded in killing a child with only three or four blows; with what satisfaction they pushed the corpse into the mother's arms!' At Treblinka, most babies were taken from their mothers on arrival, killed, and hurled into a ditch, along with invalids and cripples. Sometimes thin wails could be heard from the ditch, whose guards wore Red Cross armbands and which was known as The Infirmary.

The smashing of babies' heads reflects the extent to which the dualism of anti-Semitic violence persisted, with secret, scientific killing proceeding alongside sudden, spontaneous acts of unspeakable cruelty. Jews died in every kind of way known to depraved humanity. At the Mauthausen quarry, an Italian Jew with a good voice was made to stand on top of a rock already wired with dynamite, and then blown to death as he sang 'Ave Maria'. Hundreds of Dutch Jews were forced to jump to their deaths from the cliff overlooking the quarry, known as The Parachutist's Wall. Many thousands of Jews were flogged to death for trivial camp offences: keeping a coin or wedding ring, failing to move Jewish insignia from the clothes of the murdered, having a piece of bread from an outside bakery, drinking water without permission, smoking, poor saluting. There were even cases of beheading. Kurt Franz, deputy commandant at Treblinka, kept a pack of fierce dogs used to tear Jews to death. Sometimes the guards killed with anything that came to hand. A Belzec eye-witness testified about 'a very young boy' who had just arrived at the camp:

He was a fine example of health, strength and youth. We were surprised by his cheerful manner. He looked around and said quite happily: 'Has anyone ever escaped from here?' It was enough. One of the guards overheard him and the boy was tortured to death. He was stripped naked and hung upside down from the gallows; he hung there for three hours. He was strong and still very much alive. They took him down and laid him on the ground and pushed sand down his throat with sticks until he died.

In the end, as the Reich imploded and first Himmler, then his camp commandants, lost control, the scientific side of the Final Solution broke down or was abandoned, and the dualism merged into one insensate force: the desire, right up to the last possible moment, to kill any Jews who remained. The Sonderskommandos, the ghetto bosses, Rumkowski included, the Jewish police and SS spies – all were killed. As the front collapsed, the SS made determined efforts to march columns of Jews away from it, so they could be killed at leisure. The fanaticism with which they clung to their duties as mass murderers, long after the Third Reich was irretrievably doomed, is one of the gruesome curiosities of human history. There was one revolt of the killers. At Ebensee, a Mauthausen satellite camp and the last in German hands, the SS refused to mow down 30,000 Jews who would not march into a tunnel to be blown up. But some killings continued even after camps were liberated. British tanks took Belsen on 15 April 1945 but moved on into action, leaving Hungarian SS guards 'in partial command' for forty-eight hours. During that time they shot seventy-two Jews for such offences as taking potato-peelings from the kitchen.

So nearly six million Jews died. Two millennia of anti-Semitic hatred, of all varieties, pagan, Christian and secular, superstitious and cerebral, folk and academic, had been soldered by Hitler into one overwhelming juggernaut and then driven by his unique energy and will over the helpless body of European Jewry. There were still 250,000 Jews in displaced persons' camps, and scattered survivors everywhere. But the great Ashkenazi Jewry of eastern Europe had, in essence, been destroyed. An act of genocide had indeed been carried out. As the camps were opened and the full extent of the calamity became known, some Jews in their innocence expected an outraged humanity to comprehend the magnitude of the crime and say with one thunderous voice: this is enough. Anti-Semitism must end. We must be done with it once and for all, draw a line under this stupendous outrage, and start history afresh.

But that is not how human societies work. Nor, in particular, is it how the anti-Semitic impulse works. It is protean, assuming new forms as it consumes the old. The effect of the Holocaust was chiefly to transfer the principal focus of anti-Jewish hatred from east-central Europe to the Middle East. What worried some Arab leaders was that Hitler's solution had not, in fact, been final. On 6 May

1942, for instance, the Grand Mufti had protested to the Bulgarian government that Jews were leaving there for Palestine. They should, he said, be sent back to Poland 'under strong and energetic guard'.

Even in Europe, there was often loathing, rather than pity, for the bewildered survivors. Their very nakedness, the habits bred by their atrocious treatment, stirred new waves of anti-Semitism. Among those who yielded to revulsion was General Patton, who had charge of more Jewish DPs than any other commander. He called 'the Jewish type of DP' a 'sub-human species without any of the cultural or social refinements of our time'. No ordinary people, he said, 'could have sunk to the level of degradation these have reached in the short space of four years'. More active hostility to the pitiful survivors was shown in the countries from which they had been drawn, especially Poland. The Jewish DPs knew what awaited them. They resisted repatriation to the best of their strength. A Jewish GI from Chicago, who had to load survivors on to railroad trucks for Poland, related: 'Men threw themselves on their knees in front of me, tore open their shirts and screamed: "Kill me now!" They would say, "You might just as well kill me now, I am dead anyway if I go back to Poland." ' In some cases they were proved right. In Poland, anti-Semitic riots broke out in Cracow in August 1945 and spread to Sosnowiec and Lublin. Luba Zindel, who returned to Cracow from a Nazi camp, described an attack on her synagogue on the first Sabbath in August: 'They were shouting that we had committed ritual murders. They began firing at us and beating us up. My husband was sitting beside me. He fell down, his face full of bullets.' She tried to flee to the West but was stopped by Patton's troops. The British ambassador in Warsaw reported that anyone in Poland with a Jewish appearance was in danger. During the first seven months after the end of the war there were 350 anti-Semitic murders in Poland.

Nevertheless, in two important respects the Holocaust, by its sheer enormity, did bring a qualitative change in the way international society reacted to violence inflicted on Jews. It was universally agreed that both punishment and restitution were necessary and to some extent both were carried out. War-crime trials began at Nuremberg on 20 November 1945, with the Final Solution as a principal element in the indictment. The first trial of Nazi leaders ended on 1 October 1946, which coincided with the Day of Atonement, when twelve defendants were sentenced to death, three to life imprisonment, four to prison terms, and three were acquitted. There followed twelve major trials of Nazi criminals, known as Subsequent Nuremberg Proceedings, in four of which the planning and execution of the Final Solution were a chief element. In these twelve trials, 177 Nazis were convicted, twelve sentenced to death, twenty-five to life imprisonment, and the remainder to long prison terms. There were many further trials in each of the three Western occupation zones, nearly all of them involving atrocities against Jews. Between 1945 and 1951 a total of 5,025 Nazis were convicted, 806 being sentenced to death. But in only 486 cases was the death sentence carried out. Moreover, a Clemency Act passed in January 1951 by the US high commissioner in Germany led to the early release of many senior war criminals in US hands. The United Nations War Crimes Commission prepared lists of 36,529 'war-criminals' (including Japanese), the majority of them involved in anti-Jewish atrocities. In the first three years after the war, additional trials were held by eight Allied countries of 3,470 on the list, of whom 952 were sentenced to death and 1,905 received prison sentences.

Large numbers of national war-crimes trials were held in nearly all the states involved in the war, involving about 150,000 accused and producing over 100,000 convictions, many of them in punishment of anti-Jewish crimes. Many thousands of Nazis and their allies involved in the Final Solution were swallowed up in the Gulag Archipelago. When German courts began to function again in 1945, they too began to try war criminals, and in the first quarter-century they sentenced twelve to death, ninety-eight to life imprisonment and 6,000 to prison terms. With the creation of Israel in 1948, she also (as we shall see) was able to take part in the retributive process. The pursuit and arraignment of Nazi war criminals continues at this moment, more than fifty years after the Holocaust ended, and is likely to last another decade, at the end of which all those involved in perpetrating it will be dead or in extreme old age. No one can say that justice was done. Some of the senior executants of the Final Solution disappeared and lived out their lives in peace or at any rate in hiding. Others received or served sentences which bore no relation to their crimes. Yet equally, no one can doubt the scale of the effort made to punish those who committed history's gravest crime or the persistence with which it has been maintained.

The struggle to secure compensation for the victims produced similar mixed results. Chaim Weizmann, on behalf of the Jewish Agency, submitted a reparations claim to the four occupying powers on 20 September 1945. Nothing came of it, mainly because no general peace treaty was ever negotiated or signed. The three Western powers set aside proceeds from the sale of confiscated Nazi property for Jewish victims. But they had to make individual claims and a well-meant project turned into a bureaucratic muddle. By 1953 only 11,000 claims had been processed, yielding $83 million. In the meantime, in January 1951 the Israeli Prime Minister, David Ben Gurion, had submitted a collective claim to the federal German government for $1.5 billion, based on Israel's absorption of 500,000 refugees from Germany at a capital cost of $3,000 each. It meant negotiating directly with the Germans, something many camp survivors found unacceptable. But Ben Gurion got majority approval with his slogan: 'Let not the murderers of our people also be their heirs!' Agreement on a figure of $845 million, paid over fourteen years, was reached and, despite attempts by the Arab states to prevent ratification, came into effect in March 1953, and was duly completed in 1965. Moreover, it also provided for the passing of a federal Indemnification Law, indemnifying individual victims or their dependants for loss of life or limb, damage to health, and loss of careers, professions, pensions and insurance. It further made restitution for loss of liberty at a rate of a dollar for each day the victims were imprisoned, forced to live in a ghetto, or wear a star. Those who lost the family breadwinner received a pension, former civil servants got notional promotions and compensation was also given for loss of education. Victims could also claim for loss of property. This comprehensive settlement was administered by a staff of nearly 5,000 judges, civil servants and clerks, who by 1973 had processed over 95 per cent of 4,276,000 claims. For a quarter of a century it absorbed about 5 per cent of the federal budget. At the time of writing, about $25 billion has been paid out, and by the end of the twentieth century the figure will be over $30 billion. These payments cannot exactly be described as generous or even adequate. But they are a great deal more than Weizmann or Ben Gurion ever expected and they represent a genuine desire on the part of the federal government to pay for Germany's crime.

The rest of the reparations story is much less satisfactory. None of the German industrialists involved in the slave-labour programme ever acknowledged the smallest moral responsibility for its atrocious consequences. They argued, in defending themselves against both criminal charges and civil claims, that in the circumstances of total war the forced-labour procedure was not unlawful. They resisted compensation every legal inch of the way and behaved throughout with a striking mixture of meanness and arrogance. Friedrich Flick declared: 'Nobody of the large circle of persons who know my fellow defendants and myself will be willing to believe that we committed crimes against humanity and nothing will convince us that we are war criminals.' Flick never paid out a single deutschmark and was worth over $1,000 million when he died, aged ninety, in 1972. Altogether the German companies paid out a total of only $13 million and fewer than 15,000 Jews got a share of it. The IG Farben slave-workers at Auschwitz got $1,700 each, the AEG-Telefunken slaves $500 or less. The families of those who had been worked to death got nothing. But the behaviour of the Germans capitalists was no worse than that of the Communist successor states. The East German government never even troubled to reply to requests for compensation. Nor was there any response from Rumania. The whole vast area of oppression controlled by Communist authorities since 1945 yielded the Jews nothing whatever.

Austria's behaviour was the worst of the lot. Though the great majority of Austrians had supported the Anschluss, though nearly 550,000 out of seven million Austrians were actually Nazi Party members, though Austrians had fought alongside Germany throughout and (as we have noted) had killed nearly half the Jewish victims, the Allied declaration of November 1943 in Moscow categorized Austria as 'the first free nation to fall victim to Hitlerite aggression'. Austria was therefore exempted from reparations at the post-war Potsdam Conference. Thus legally absolved, all the Austrian political parties entered into an agreement to evade moral responsibility too, and to claim the status of victim. As the Austrian Socialist Party put it (1946): 'It is not Austria that should make restitution. Rather, it is to Austria that restitution should be made.' Austria was obliged by the Allies to pass a war criminal law, but did not even establish a prosecuting body to enforce it until 1963. Even so, many were amnestied by decree and those trials that did take place usually produced acquittals. Jews claiming compensation were told to apply to Germany, unless they could actually identify their former property in Austria itself; and very few indeed got as much as $1,000.

There was a belated but nevertheless welcome attempt to make moral reparation by the Christian churches. Both Catholic and Lutheran anti-Semitism had contributed, over many centuries, to the Jew-hatred which culminated in Hitlerism. Neither church had behaved well during the war. Pope Pius XII, in particular, had failed to condemn the Final Solution, though he knew of it. One or two isolated voices had been raised on behalf of the Jews. Fr Bernhard Lichtenberg, from St Hedwig's Catholic Cathedral in Berlin, had publicly prayed for the Jews in 1941. His apartment was searched and notes found for an undelivered sermon in which he planned to tell his congregation that they should not believe in a Jewish conspiracy to kill all Germans. For this he served a two-year sentence and on his release was ordered to Dachau. This seems the only case of its kind. Among eye-witnesses of the *Judenrazzia* in Rome on 16 October 1943 was a Jesuit priest, Augustin Bca, who came from Baden in Germany and acted as Pius XII's confessor. Twenty years later, during the Second Vatican Council, he had the chance, as head of the Secretariat for

Christian Unity, to quash, once and for all, the ancient accusation of deicide against the Jews. He took charge of the council *schema*, 'On the Jews', enlarged it into a 'Declaration of the Relations of the Church to Non-Christian Religions', taking in Hinduism, Buddhism and Islam as well as Judaism, and successfully steered it through the council, which adopted it in November 1965. It was a grudging document, less forthright than Bea had hoped, making no apology for the church's persecution of the Jews, and inadequate acknowledgment of the contribution of Judaism to Christianity. The key passage read: 'True the Jewish authorities and those who followed their lead pressed for the death of Christ; still, what happened in his passion cannot be charged against the Jews of today. Although the Church is the new people of God, the Jews should not be represented as rejected of God or accursed, as if this followed from the Holy Scriptures.' This was not much. But it was something. In view of the fierce opposition it aroused, it might even be considered a great deal. Moreover, it was part of a much more general process whereby the civilized world was attempting to strike at the institutional supports of anti-Semitism.

That was welcome. But the Jews had grasped that the civilized world, however defined, could not be trusted. The overwhelming lesson the Jews learned from the Holocaust was the imperative need to secure for themselves a permanent, self-contained and above all sovereign refuge where if necessary the whole of world Jewry could find safety from its enemies. The First World War made the Zionist state possible. The Second World War made it essential. It persuaded the overwhelming majority of Jews that such a state had to be created and made secure whatever the cost, to themselves or to anyone else.